The Little Book of Iron Age Skills 2

by Will Llawerch

This booklet edition 2022.

First Published in United Kingdom by Badger Print 2020
This edition published by Endeavour Productions Ca 2022
For Amazon

Sponsored By: www.ironageguru.com & www.kelticos.org

Table of Contents

Timeline: 250 BC – 84AD
Who, What, When & Where?

The Iron Age people referred to in this book are Britons and Gauls.

The Gauls were the inhabitants of what is now modern France and belonged to a group of people whom archaeologists call 'The Celts'.

This term, 'The Celts' has been misleading and many people today think that the inhabitants of Britain and Ireland were Celts. However, it is now generally accepted that the Britons and Gauls were different cultural groups but whom both understood iron production and traded with one another.

When the Roman's spoke of the Gaul's, Gallia or Celtae they were referring to different tribes of people who stretched from the North of Italy to France, from southern Germany to parts of Spain.

We know that the basis for their language was shared but had many regional dialects, they worshipped the same God's and Goddesses, but each tribe used variations on the names of these deities.

Britons and those Iron Age people in Ireland are thought to have been descendants of the Bronze Age farmers and earlier who had lived in Britain and Ireland since the Stone Age or before the water levels rose and separated them from the European continent. The Romans tell us that they too considered the Britons to be separate from Gauls; however, Caesar describes trade between the south east of Britain and the Gauls and notes that in those areas the communities were very similar.

The descendants of those Britons today, are the people who live and have ancestors in Scotland, Wales, Cornwall, Ireland, Brittany and the Isle of Man.

So, for the purposes of this book, by Iron Age people I mean both Britons and Gauls.

What did Iron Age Animals look like?

Lots of books tell us about Celtic warriors and Druids and some show us many of the artefacts that have survived two thousand years and which we can now look at in Museums. But perhaps one part of the living history aspect that is still with us are the animals that the Iron Age people would have known. Even now, in the first half of the 21st century if we are lucky, we can still see some of the animals that the Iron Age people took for granted. Though today many are now on endangered lists, their future for the next 2000 years with regret is uncertain.

So what kind of animals can we see today that were common sights in the Iron Age?

All through the earlier Bronze Age, as early farmers began to replace the hunter gatherer lifestyles, Sheep have been very useful creatures to domesticate. Not only does their wool give you warm clothing; they provide meat to eat and bone to carve. You can even make soap from the lanolin in their wool. By the Iron Age in Europe, there were different breeds of sheep. The Mouflon in particular would have been a common sight in Gaul and Europe.

Fig. 1

The Mouflon is one of the oldest breeds of sheep in the world.

Soay Sheep

The Soay sheep are named after the Island of Soay off the coast of Scotland. This breed of sheep is arguably the oldest in the British Isles and there would have been many of them in the Iron Age landscape. A small sheep, often confused by people who have never seen them before for a goat, the Soay roam free and it is practically impossible to fence them in. Their wool is very fine which adds strength to the suggestion that the woolen cloaks and clothes woven in Britain was very fine and the Romans appreciated its quality.

Fig. 2 (left) & 3 (below)

Manx Loaghtan

The Manx Loaghtan comes from the Isle of Man between the coast of Ireland and United Kingdom. During the Iron Age, flocks of these sheep could even be found in the north west of Britain. The strange name is Manx Gaelic and refers to the colour of the sheep naming them 'Brown as a mouse'. As late as the 1800's this breed of sheep was available in white and black also, however it is the brown from which its name derives that is left. One of the most recognizable characteristics of the Manx Loaghtan is the four or sometimes six horns found on the males. Though like the Soay sheep, both Ewes (females) and Rams (males) grow horns. The Ewe's horns are smaller.

Fig. 4
Manx Loaghten Sheep.

Fig. 5
A male and female Manx Loaghten.

Cattle

Fig. 6
A Dexter.

We lost the original Ancient British Cow centuries ago. But today, the Dexter cattle are the closest surviving breed to the Iron Age cattle.

A chieftain based much of his wealth on how many head of cattle the tribe owned. Undoubtedly, these cattle were used for labour either as a team for the Ard or for heavy lifting and pulling of sleds. It would be the 1700's in Europe and North America before horses began to replace oxen and cattle as regular draft animals.

Ponies

Measuring on average no more than 14 hands high, it is generally agreed that the Exmoor pony is the oldest native breed still available in Britain. They are tenacious and rugged and can still be seen wild in parts of South Wales and Cornwall.

Fig. 7
A Welsh Mountain Pony.

However another ancient breed of horse is also still with us, unfortunately now on the critical list of endangered, the Eriskay Pony is a little smaller than the Exmoor at 13.5 hands, but just as wild as the hills of Scotland from which it is said to have been in use by the Ancient Britons and later the Picts and Vikings. In the 1970's only 20 Eriskay ponies were left, but thanks to the Eriskay Pony Society, there are now 420 in existence.

Fig. 8
An Eriskay Pony

Pigs & Wild boar

The original ancestor of the Berkshire pig was brown in colour with black patches. The sow gives a lot of milk which means its piglets gain weight easily. They are great outdoor pigs and easy to look after. Excellent for Iron Age farms.

The wild boar is the icon animal of the Iron Age, more so than the horse for the amount of times it is represented in artwork, carvings and mythology of the Iron Age Celts. From 18 months to two years old, the boars start to grow their tusks.

The male can grow to almost 500lbs in weight and although they are very domestic and family-oriented animals in the company of their sows and piglets, they can be ferocious when roused or surprised by people out for a walk in the forest.

Fig. 9 (above) & 10 (below)
A Berkshire Pig.

That's probably why the warriors liked to spike their hair with a lime wash to resemble this brave fearsome animal.

Badgers

The badger

In the Iron Age, as now, the Badger is a solitary animal preferring to come out at night. If you want any chance of seeing one, first and last light is your best bet.

Like later rabbits which came with the Romans, the badger likes to live underground, sometimes at the base of trees in the woods. With their short legs and large claws, the badger doesn't run very fast and its den or hole in the ground is its defence. However, if attacked, a badger will bite and lock its jaw on you to the bitter end.

Fig. 11
A pair of badgers.

In the 21st Century, badgers are an endangered species but in the Iron Age, when badgers were more common, they must have been a regular sight for farmers. The badger eats practically everything it can from what it finds on the forest floor to fish and raw meat. In parts of modern France, badgers are tamed and used to sniff out truffles from the forest floor. Truffles are in demand in many good French restaurants.

The Brown Hare

Of all the animals, with the exception of the wild boar perhaps, the wild hare is one of the most enduring symbols. The Latin name for the hare is *Lepus europaeus*. To the Iron Age people, the hare was a sacred animal that they kept for pleasure and never hunted. We know that the Iceni Queen, Boudicca is said to have opened a sack and allowed a captured hare to run free from it as a sign of the forthcoming battle with Rome.

Unfortunately, we don't know which way the hare ran. We do; however, know that Boudicca lost the battle.

So, what's the difference between a rabbit and a Hare?

A Hare lives on the ground in a 'form' or nest. A rabbit lives underground in a warren.

In its defense, a hare can run as fast as 45 miles per hour and a rabbit can't.

The hare is bigger than a rabbit, has longer, larger ears and doesn't have a fluffy white tail.

The hare feeds on grass in the summer months and twigs and buds in winter. In the spring of the year, Hares can be seen "boxing" in the open meadows. Unless the Druids knew better, it was probably thought in the Iron Age, that the males were boxing to see who was strongest.

However, we now know it's the female telling a young male that she's not ready to breed yet.

Fig. 12
The Wild Hare.

Like so many of Europe's indigenous species, the hare is declining all over Europe. Their natural habitats are being changed as more country-side becomes urban and more chemicals and new farming techniques are used by farmers.

Fig. 13
The Wild Hare.

How to Make Iron Age Paint.

Fig. 14
La Tene Style 5 art in natural colours.

Iron oxides are commonly found in Iron Ore mines. However, in the Iron Age, before the Romans arrived, underground mines were not as common as open caste mines. This means, that the ore could be seen on the surface and dug from the ground as it naturally occurred. Depending on the geology present, different colours would appear as veins or strata in the rock.

Some colours are soft veins, which mean you can run your finger along them and the colour will be left on your finger. The darker colours need a chisel to hammer them out. Ochre Red is not the only colour to come from Iron Oxide, Mustard yellow, Purple and dark brown are all available depending on the strata of ore collected.

After collecting the colours you want, pestle and mortar the oxide into a powder and mix together with ½ cup of white chalk, 2 teaspoons of honey and 1 cup of linseed oil. Remember to add the honey last.

There is an excellent spread with this mix and 1 tablespoon of pigment will cover four, man-sized shields. By mixing paints, you can create different colours including orange and black. Interestingly enough, copper mines also offer different colours of strata and the possibility of the Britons painting themselves with this sort of paint offers an interesting comparison with archaeological evidence.

Fig. 15

In the 1980's, a bog body was discovered at Lindow Moss in England. During their research, archaeologists noted that the body bore high levels of metal oxides in the mud around the skin. So, if the Britons were not tattooing with woad. They may have been simply painting themselves.

You'll need some wooden bowls and a paint brush; a larger mixing bowl is a good idea too. Here are some photos to show you how to make the paint. It takes quite a long time to dry but is still practical even after 2000 years.

Fig. 16 (top left), 17 (top right) & 18 (left)
Examples of Paint and Artwork in Iron Age
Society.

Fig. 19
1/Each bowl contains a colour of fine ground oxide. You need a lump of chalk and a bowl of linseed oil.

Fig. 20
2/With a pestle grind the flakes of chalk into a fine powder.

Fig. 21

3/With your chalk finely powdered, its time to start mixing the ingredients.

Fig. 22

4/ Add your choice of colour to the chalk. Only add one colour at a time. You'll have to follow this process for each colour.!

Fig. 23

5/ Mix the oxide and chalk together.

Fig. 24

6/ Next add some linseed oil and prepare to mix into a paint consistency.

Fig. 25
7/ The finer you ground the oxide and chalk right now the better.

Fig. 26
8/ Add some more linseed oil until you get a suitable paint texture. Add a small amount of honey. Too much and your paint will turn globby.

Fig. 27

9/ *Paint your shield, roundhouse, chariot whatever you wish. Drying times can be quite long, leave overnight.*

Fig. 28 (left) & 29 (right)
A warrior with a Iron Age shield painted with natural ochre colours in La Tene style 5 art.

Herbs & Medicine

Today, many people like to use herbs either in the kitchen or to treat minor ailments. But few remember that at one time or another, across all the continents as far back as the Stone Age, people in antiquity have been using all sorts of different species of plants for the very same reasons.

In fact, by the Iron Age, the knowledge of how to use herbs for medicine and cooking was intrinsic in the day to day lives of the people. Perhaps it could even be described as a general knowledge amongst all levels of people.

It is difficult to tell whether the Iron Age peoples grouped all the herbs together in formal gardens (like the Romans did) or whether instead those in need made journey's out into the landscape around them to look for naturally growing herbs each time they need them.

In my opinion, I think though the general population had a general knowledge of what some plants were good for, it would be a smaller section of society who specialized in the subject. These people may have been older women, perhaps midwives who knew exactly where particular medicinal herbs grew and would hold a small stock in the form of ointments, teas, poultices. In turn, the inhabitants of communities would go to them directly in times of need.

Fig. 30

Herb	Remedy
Apple cider vinegar	Acne
Artichoke	Lowers Cholesterol
Bilberry	Good for eyes & diabetes
Cranberry	Bladder Infections
Chamomile	Insomnia
Comfrey	Stomach Ulcers & intestinal tracts
Dandelion	Digestive
Dill and Dill oil	Colon health & flatulence
Elderberry	A & B influenza
Fennel	Insect bites & food poisoning
Feverfew	Migraines
Garlic	Antibiotic
Ginger	Calms Upset stomach & Nerves
Goldenseal	Urinary Tract Infections
Hawthorn	High& low Blood pressure & Gallstones
Hibiscus	Antibacterial
Honey	Antibacterial. Good for dry coughs & small cuts.
Liquorice	Good for Cough's & lungs
Marjoram	Chilblains & Sore Throats
Oregano	Antibacterial
Parsley	Bad Breath & Purifies blood
Peppermint	Settles bowels
Plantain	Insect bites, heat rashes & eczema
St. John's Wort	Anti-depressant
Sweet sage	Bronchial Spasms
Wormwood	Kills parasites & good for digestion

Fig. 31
Madder

Fig. 32
Wild Garlic

Fig. 33
Sage

Fig. 34
Woad

What did the Iron Age people eat in winter?

Salting, Drying, Storing

The Iron Age people didn't have electricity so preserving was the only way they could ensure they had food through the winter

Salt-cured meat or salted meats, like bacon or kippered fish, was a way of preserving or curing meat in salty brine. Salted meat and fish are still commonly eaten as a staple of the diet today in many parts of the world.

Fig. 35

How did it work?

Salt helped stop the growth of microorganisms and killed unwanted bacteria which would otherwise have made the food unfit to eat.

One of the oldest recipes for salting was to half fill a barrel with 1 cup salt for every 4.4 litres of hot water. That's about 34 parts water - 1-part salt plus a little vinegar.

Before placing meat into the barrel, the Ancients would have cut and jointed the meat into manageable ham sized pieces. Next, they would have soaked the meat in the barrel for a week, 7 days.

When they removed the meat from the barrel, they would have dried it off with a cloth and kept it covered to ensure it didn't attract flies. Next it was time to hang it up in a cool dry place to dry. If they were successful, the meat would keep for a minimum of 5 weeks in hot weather. During winter, the meat remained edible for two months or more.

Most importantly, if they didn't get it right, it will be very obvious quite quickly.

When they were ready to eat the meat, they rinsed the salt out by placing the meat in a tub of water and kneading the meat to force out the excess salt. They probably had to do these two or three times, pour out the water and repeat again.

Drying:

Drying is arguably the oldest method of food preservation known to man. Drying was a very simple way to preserve food. It didn't need salt, vinegar, sugar or anything else. Depending on the time of year in which the Iron Age people prepared their food for winter storage, all they needed was either sunshine or a warm, dry place so that the fruit or vegetables could lose all their moisture. Drying was a simple way to stop harmful Bacteria growing.

The Iron Age people would have known the art of drying wild fruits, fish and meats to ensure they had enough food through the wintertime.

Fig. 36

Icelandic Fish being dried the traditional way.

The number one rule when drying was to choose fruits, vegetables and herbs in top quality condition. If the Britons and Gauls had attempted to dry half-rotten, overripe or wilted picks, the food would spoil before the drying process could take place.

Food would be sliced, diced or chopped uniformly so it could dry properly. If some slices were thicker than others, half the batch would have over-dried by the time the other half was ready. Fruits and vegetables would have been sliced about 1/4 inch thin for drying. Or a fine dice or medium chop can be used depending on pick ensured uniform size and cut down on drying times.

Archaeology tells us that most Iron Age villages, farmsteads had access to granaries. These structures are perfect for allowing air to circulate around and under the food. Though there is no such evidence, an educated guess supposes that linen may have been hung up, around the food inside the granaries to ensure flies can't get in, but the air can still circulate. The linen also would help trap moisture in the air.

The fact that we find evidence of numerous granaries on Iron Age sites suggests that each held different food stuffs in storage and may have featured racks at different levels as opposed to food hanging from the ceiling.

It is unlikely that these dried foods were stored in subterranean cellars as dampness ruin the food and caused bacteria or mould to grow. When I tried this, I found that leaving them strung up also brings the nuisance of mice, rats and squirrels into your house. Earthenware pottery jars with close fitting lids are good.

Reconstituting Food

Fig. 37
Reconstituting seaweed.

Fruit and vegetables could be reconstituted before using by soaking in cold water until they plumped back up.

Dried vegetables could also be added directly to soups, stews, or other dishes that required cooking the dried goods without presoaking. Also dried vegetables could be added directly to soups and stews.

Occasionally, we have found Pestle and Mortars on Iron Age sites and its no coincidence that the dried preserves taste great when powdered using a mortar and pestle and sprinkled on food.

Raspberries, Blueberries, Gooseberries, Wild strawberries, Rhubarb, Carrots, Onions, Green Peas, Mushrooms and Garlic are just some of the things that the Britons & Gauls could dry.

Fig. 38
A Granary Building.

On all Iron Age sites, archaeologists find evidence of numerous small structures which may have looked like the granary pictured above. It's an educated guess but these structures, similar to those still being used in modern Spain and Portugal would be perfect for drying and preserving food.

How to prepare and spin a fleece Iron Age Style.

Mouflon and Soay fleeces do not need shearing; instead their wool coat in the Iron Age would be plucked by hand. But if you have ever seen fleece fresh from the sheep, it's very smelly and dirty. So, how do you clean a fleece?

Once the wool is collected it will need to be washed twice in hot water. However, as we all know, if you get wool too hot for too long, you end up with felt. So, instead of boiling the fleece, you need to immerse it on cold water in a large cauldron over an open fire. It's best to do this outside if you can.

Feed the fire with regular amounts of wood being careful not to raise the temperature too quickly. Slowly bring the water up to boiling point and then put the fire out. Do this by raking the logs away. If you use water, it will just place lots of ash into your water filled Cauldron!

Next, let the water return to a cold temperature naturally. Pour the dirty water out and do it again, this time, put a very small amount of detergent in with the fleece and slowly, infrequently stir it. Do the same thing, bring it up to a high temperature and then let it cool down naturally.

Fig. 39
Unprocessed sheep's fleece.

This will clean your fleece without stripping it of its lanolin content.

Stretch the fleece out and let it air dry. This should be all you need to do before breaking down the fibres ready to drop spin into thread.

Fig. 40
Washed & cleaned before carding.

Then, once dry enough to handle, you can take handfuls of the wool and pull it apart gently with your hands until it resembles a big fluffy cloud.

Whilst you are breaking the fleece down and stretching the fibres, you will be able to remove any remaining pieces of twig or leaves.

The next step is to create a thread using a drop spindle. Using a drop spindle is easy and lets you, with a bit of practice produce a fine piece of thread which can be woven on a loom.

The way the drop spindle works is, you allow gravity to put tension on the thread and by rotating the top of the spindle with your finger & thumb before letting go, you can then control the twist on the fibres with one hand and feed new fibres out with the other.

It takes a bit of practice because when you just get the hang of it, the drop spindle needs to be spun again. But after lots of practice, you will find that it becomes second nature and you'll be able to talk to people whilst spinning.

Finally, once spun, the threads can be woven into cloth using a warp weighted loom for clothes and trade.

Fig. 41
Here, a young Iron Age Girl creates thread with her drop spindle.

How to dye using natural pigments

Fig. 42
Natural Dyes, madder root, cochineal and woad.

In the past, there has been debate amongst scholars and historians about the natural colours that were available to dye cloth within the Iron Age. A big part of this discussion is because not very much cloth survives from the Iron Age. The pieces that do survive are woolen and mostly come from waterlogged conditions. They show us that the Iron Age people were able to produce fairly complicated plaids, stripes and solid coloured clothes using a variety of weaves including tabbeyweave and hounds tooth patterns. But few surviving examples of textile actually hold their original colours.

Fixing the colour requires a mordent and in the Iron Age one of the best-known mordents was salt.

Further still, there has been much discussion around whether the Britons and Gauls were able to produce a solid black colour. Well, we know that they had the plants required to do so, such as woad for blue, madder for red and a brilliant yellow most likely from the weld plant. So, it is possible. Yellow can be found in many plants and can be quite bright, although because the Iron Age people did not have modern chemicals to fix the colour permanently, the colours eventually faded within a year or so.

It's also worth remembering that linen is more difficult to dye than wool and so one can imagine the linen undershirts being left its natural hue.

However, black has the strange attribute which, when added to reproduction clothes from the Iron Age, to the modern eye, looks too anachronistic. In other words, it looks too modern and so up until fairly recently, black was the one obtainable natural colour that re-enactors of the period chose not to use. Though today all of these colours are easily obtainable, it seems that in the Iron Age, the fact that a person was able to wear colourful clothes, above the earthy greens and browns suggests they had to have a certain level of wealth in the tribe in order to do so.

If you could afford colour, then yellows, various shades of blue and brick red were also fairly common. However, in my opinion, colour is only part of the picture. I believe that the higher status you were, then the finer the weave of the cloth and perhaps the more complicated the pattern woven into it that you could afford to buy and have your clothes made from. One Roman writer describes the Gaulish High Society as having gold thread shot through their clothes.!

WOAD is a biannual plant and so, you plant a crop in the first year and a second crop the next year. This ensures a yearly supply. The Indigo blue hue is created by fermenting the first yield of leaves.

MADDER comes from the roots of the madder plant. The roots produce a red dye when mulched up and boiled. A beetroot-like hue can be obtained as well as lighter shades depending on the strength of the dye and the length of time you process the wool in it.

WELD is another plant and, like madder must be boiled to extract the Yellow dye. However, it is the whole plant that must be used.

Remember you don't have to weave only using a warp weighted loom. You can make tablet woven borders with cards and also more complicated patterns on treddle looms. On the next page, you can see some examples of not only naturally dyed wool using onion skins, grass and bark, but also a modern reconstruction of a genuine length of woven wool found in Hallstatt, Austria. Also, you can see that in my opinion, linen shirts were not left blank, but stitched with bright designs, In this case emmer wheat motif from coins.

Fig. 43 (above)
Natural Earth Colours.

Fig. 44 (above)
Hallstatt Reconstructed tablet weave by Terry & Cindy Sebolt.

Fig. 45 (above)
A upright Warp weighted loom.

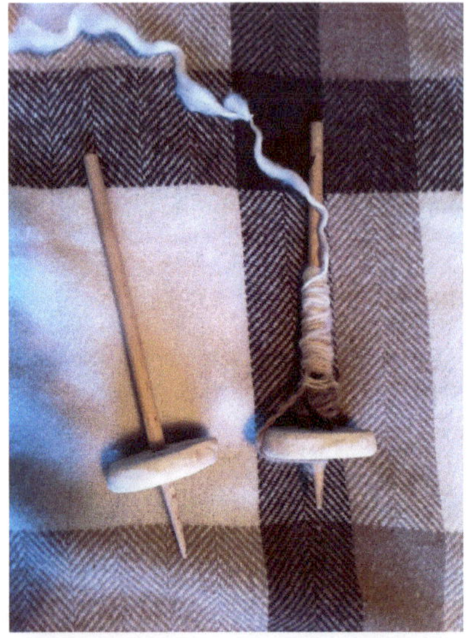

The end result, the sheep's wool is sheared and washed, spun and dyed, before being hung on a warp-weighted loom where it will be woven into cloth. Here you can see examples of natural colours, Woad blue, Madder & Weld/Woad green.

Fig. 46 (left)
A Pair of Iron Age Reproduction Drop Spindles.

Fig. 47 (above)

Farming Methods

Throughout the earlier Bronze Age, the populations of what would become Celtic Britain & Europe remained fairly small but constant. Before the discovery and use of Iron, farming techniques had been fairly basic with Bronze Age ploughs creating nothing more than a shallow groove in light upland soils. The remains of these early field systems can still be seen occasionally. They look like faint, long, thin rectangles on the upper slopes of valleys in parts of UK.

We know that from the mid 2nd century BC, The Iron Age farmers began to use the iron plough share and crop rotation. They probably were well acquainted with animal dung as a fertilizer.

The Celtic plough is fitted with a knife-like blade which cuts into the soil whilst the plough share turns the soil.

This was a brilliant idea by the Iron Age farmers because there were a

Fig. 48 (above) & 49 (right)
A reconstructed Ard (plough).

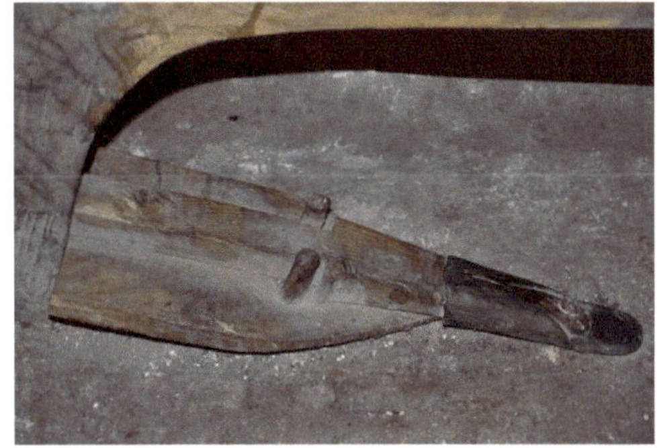

lot of tired hard-working farmers in the Bronze Age who had had to plough their fields twice because they didn't have this new feature.

We know the Iron Age peoples were using this new iron plough share technology because archaeologists have found traces of the score marks, they left in ancient field layers.

The Iron Age farmers were so clever they even invented a harvester on two wheels which looks like a cross between half a wooden box and a digger bucket with carved teeth on the lower edge.

We think it was designed to push against the crop, say emmer wheat were the stalk meets the husk, the teeth and the forward push of the box cut the heads off the crop. It was so good, the Romans started using it.

We know that populations grow at times when food is plentiful and it would be the introduction of the iron plowshare which was responsible for allowing Iron Age farmers to maximize their use of the land.

The name of the Iron Age Plough was an 'Ard'. With its iron plowshare, pulled behind a team of oxen, the development of cultivated land with heavier soils and clay became possible.

Around the same time as this dynamic new development in farming, new species of crops were introduced into Britain.

Farmers would continue to plough in long thin fields so that they didn't have to turn their teams of oxen repeatedly. Oxen are great to plough with, however even with a lot of patience and practice; there is a lot of land wastage on the edges of your field because of the large turning maneuver needed when you have two oxen weighing close to 2000lbs each. This is something that became much easier in the 18th Century when horses were worked for the first time. So, the longer and thinner the field, the less turns you had to make and the less land you wasted.

Just like in the early 20th Century, once the field had been ploughed, the farmer would broadcast the seeds by hand. This meant walking up and down the field with a large heavy bag full of seeds. Each handful would be cast away from the farmer in a left to right, right to left motion. Once all the seeds had been sown, the farmer would rake the earth to cover the seeds and wait for the crop to grow.

There were no supermarkets like we enjoy today, and so the farmer's crop was very important. Without it, whole settlements would starve. Looking after the seeds was so important to life that in medieval times, young people were sent out into the fields with slings to scare the birds away from eating the seeds. In the Iron Age it would have been the same.

We know the Britons were very clever farmers because in the 3rd Century BC a writer named Pytheas sailed around the coast of Britain and described the farmers as very skilled.

In fact, in Britain alone, the farmers were so good, it has been stated that after the Roman invasion of Britain in 43AD, it would be almost 2000 years before the same amount of land was under the plough. As farming became so successful, populations increased dramatically, and it was this fact that brought the Celtic culture to its zenith.

How to use a fire bow

Fig. 50
Using a firebow.

From the dawn of human history, there have been many ways of starting a fire. In the beginning, Stone Age hunter gatherers were at the mercy of lightening strikes or flash points caused by dry vegetation in very hot temperatures to cause fire. By the Iron Age not only was iron and flint first used to create a spark, there was still the old way of the fire bow.

If you plan on having a go at using a fire bow to kindle a fire you will need to spend time and forethought planning all the necessary items required not only for the bow, but the actual fire too.

You will need to collect and store fresh tinder and kindling. I make my tinder from moss, bracket mushroom and birch bark. It needs to be as dry as possible. Some of my tinder is 3 years old and works incredibly well; especially the birch bark.

Remember, the ancients knew that green wood causes far too much smoke and doesn't burn well. So, they would have stored ready cut wood in a dry place for 6 months to a year before using it. This time in storage allowed the wood to season or dry out. Seasoned wood not only burns easier but burns hotter and quicker with less smoke.

Once you have your tinder collected and dried, next, with an axe, split your logs into two sizes. Thin strips for kindling. Larger logs for the main fuel.

With a pile of kindling sticks beside the hearth, you may also want to fill a small basket with charcoal flakes. I always keep a small stash of tinder drying in a large leather pouch under the low table beside the hearth.

The Fire: First, collect a small amount of tinder, about the size of your two fists held side by side, your tinder should not be squashed together too tightly, you need room for airflow. Place it beside your first few strips of kindling.

The fire bow:

A length of leather lace, or sinew measuring approx 16 inches long. You will tie it to either end of the bow so that it resembles a small archery bow.

Palm holder: You will need to cut out a flat round palm holder which is big enough to fit in the palm of your hand snugly. An indentation will be bored into the centre of this. The top end of the upright spindle will be placed in the hole. Lard or tallow should be used to lubricate the running action of the spindle.

Fireboard. The fireboard is a small length, about 10 inches long by ½ inch thick by 2 inches wide. The fireboard doesn't have to be quite so long, but I prefer it this length because I can place my foot over it to keep in steady whilst using the drill. Make a shallow indentation in the end of the fireboard and cut a clean 'V' shape into the side with the apex of the V in the centre of your indentation.

Fire Bow: A longer piece of sapling approx 24 inches long. This is going to be your bow and when bent into shape, it will give you a good 12-inch length to roll the spindle back and forth with.

Spindle: The upright stick should measure approx 12 inches long by ½ inch wide and you will need to round off one end more than the other. The thicker your stick, the looser you will have to have the cord on the bow, otherwise you won't get it looped in correctly and it will fly out and smack you in the face.

Fig. 51
The firebow.

How to use it: Place the bottom end of the spindle in the indentation on the fireboard; place the palm holder on the top of the spindle. This locks the spindle in place.

As you begin to move the bow back and forth, you will find it easier to use if you keep the bow level with the ground when moving it back and forth. If you find that the spindle is loose and hard to control, you can try to squeeze the string against the bow to give more friction.

It is not easy to use the fire bow, and you will find that it takes time to practice becoming proficient enough to trust it as a working skill. The whole apparatus may at first fall apart in your hands. However, through continued practice you will soon be able to sit and saw the bow back and forth rotating the central upright stick.

The greater your precision with the bow and spindle, it will be a matter of minutes before the fine sawdust starts to darken. Once you see the sawdust darken, a faint wisp of smoke will soon follow. As soon as you see a good pile of black sawdust and the smoke starts to appear freely, stop using the bow, remove the fireboard and catch the burning embers onto the slate underneath it. Then start to blow gently until the embers become a bright spark. Now it is time to add it to your tinder and start to either blow gently or waft the tinder containing the spark back and forth in the air to introduce oxygen. Soon a flame appears, and this is added to your tinder and kindling.

Fig. 52
The firebow in action.

Building Construction Techniques

By the Iron Age, the British style of wooden roundhouse was already old and well used. Even Late stone Age houses were probably circular and remained the same through the Bronze Age. However, how do we know that British Iron Age People had Roundhouses? Well, one of the few pieces of evidence that Archaeologists are circular patterns in the ground where long gone posts once stood. Since the 1960's, experimental archaeology particularly at Butser Ancient Farm in Hampshire, UK has devised some useful theories about construction techniques in the Iron Age.

Fig. 53

Typically, they had walls made of either stone or of wooden posts joined by wattle-and-daub panels constructed of uprights with fresh green hazel or willow woven in between.

It is generally accepted that the houses featured a conical thatched roof with a 45 degree pitch to ensure drainage when it rains. Too much water standing in the Thatch would rot the material and grow mould, On average thee structures ranged in size from less than 5m in diameter to over 15m.

Fig. 54
Examples of Iron Age Roundhouse at Butser Ancient Farm.

We don't know how people lived in them, but we get a hint from both primary & literary archaeology which suggests the interior was split half and half between day and night activities and quartered,

Fig. 55
Inside the Chieftain's house.

with evidence of different activities taking place within set areas.

In the photo above, we see quite an ornate suggested reproduction for an Iron Age village. Perhaps a Chieftains' house? A great Hall? Actually, even today, we have no real idea whether the biggest house was the meeting house, the chief's palace, or whether all the warriors lived in it, or all the mothers with children, or an extended family of Grandparents, Parents, Children & Grand Children.

Many such houses had earth floors. Some may have had floorboards. The Romans describe the floor inside covered with sheepskins and that Celts preferred to sit on the

Fig. 56 (above) & 57 (right)

floor rather than having chairs.

The roof was thatched with long river reeds. The apex formed a space which filled with smoke whilst

constantly percolating out through the thatch. The lack of oxygen in the rafters stopped the house burning down from sparks in the fire. It was a safety feature.

On the right we see an example of hazel or willow woven and covered with a mixture of clay, straw and animal manure, though in my opinion, the manure is simply a by product of the way the ancients made animals mix the clay

Fig. 58 (right)
An example of Wattle and Daub.

& straw together as they walked around a central pole 360 degrees mixing the daub with their feet.

Below we see a handful of Roundhouses in their original locations at Castell Henllys, Wales UK.

Fig. 59
The reconstructed Iron Age village in Pembrokeshire West Wales.

Here we see an example of carpentered doors. We know that it was practical to have doors and we find tools which suggest such things could be produced.

Fig. 60

One of the most recent Large diameter Roundhouse reconstructions in the last 20 years has been the "Chieftain's Hut" at Castell Henllys, Iron Age Fort in West Wales, UK. Whereas traditional reconstructions have been formed around double rings, inner and outer of concentric circles supporting the roof, this building used a wooden version of a "Keystone" principle with the weight of the rafters supporting each other and giving a wide-open interior. The largest House in the reconstructed site has been in my opinion, perhaps been erroneously referred to as the Chieftain's hut. I would put forward the hypothesis that it would be a far more practical farming level, to put all the animals in there during the winter months if not every evening. I feel that by interpreting the site as an Iron Age defended Farmstead, the wealth of the farm, its cattle & pigs would rely on this building as a big barn. I would argue this is a far more practical building than just being a chieftain's hut.

Conclusion

Today, we refer to many of the skills in this and other similar books as 'old skills', or 'survival skills' However, perhaps its more accurate to say that on a planet that has seen its population increase by 5 billion in only 60 years, there are a lot of people who show no interest in using these life skills because life has become so much easier through improvements in healthcare and technology.

Many of the skills described in my books took tens of thousands of years to evolve, for humans to learn and use, adapt and thrive on. Yet within two generations, we have, as a society thrown away this invaluable gift.

When we are making demands on a planet that cannot replace its natural resources as quickly as we are using them, in which clean water is becoming sparser and the climate more destructive....we need to remember what our Iron Age ancestors knew, when the lights go out.

Acknowledgments & Useful Links.

Castell Henllys Iron Age Fort

Pembrokeshire National Park, Wales UK

Eriskay Pony Society – Protecting & Promoting Scotland's Ancient Hebri-
dean Ponies

Eceni Wells Iron Age Village

St Fagan's Welsh Folk Museum

Llawerch Productions Ltd

www.ironageguru.com

The Iron Age Forum Online: www.kelticos.org

Butser Ancient Farm, Hampshire UK

Mouflon Photo courtesy of: Paloma Blanca Ranch as a Texas Hill Country
ranch that raises Mouflons along with other Texas exotics, including
Axis deer and white tail deer for hunts and sale. For more information
please visit: www.palomablancaranch.com.

Manx Loaghtan Sheep Breeders' Group,
http://www.manxloaghtansheep.org.

National Iron Age Museum, Andover, Hampshire. Hampshire County
Council.

Jane Russ of the Hare Preservation Trust

www.soaysheepsociety.org.uk

Image Credits

Courtesy of Alexey Ayifer
Fig. 15, 17

Courtesy of Butser Ancient Farm & Pembrokeshire National Park.
Fig. 56-57

Courtesy of Butser Ancient Farm, Hampshire UK.
Fig. 45, 53-54

Courtesy of Caroline Walker
Fig. 4-5

Courtesy of eriskaypony.org

    Fig. 8

Courtesy of Flicker

    Fig. 36

Courtesy of Food Print

    Fig. 37

Courtesy of Harbor Fish Market

    Fig. 35

Courtesy of ironageguru.com

    Fig. 16, 19-29, 39-44, 46-47, 50-51

Courtesy of iStockivandzyuba

    Fig. 30

Courtesy of Liz Furneaux

    Fig. 7

Courtesy of Llawerch Productions

    Fig. 6, 11

Courtesy of Paloma Blanca Ranch, Texas - palomablancaranch.com

    Fig. 1

Courtesy of Paul Hall Designs

    Fig. 9-10

Courtesy of Pembrokeshire National Park

    Fig. 18, 31-34, 55, 58-60

Courtesy of Skilled Survival

    Fig. 52

Courtesy of soaysheep.org

    Fig. 2-3

Courtesy of St Fagan's Folk Museum, Wales

    Fig. 14

Courtesy of St Fagan's Museum of Welsh Life

    Fig. 38

Courtesy of The Iron Age Museum in Andover, Hampshire County Council

    Fig. 48-49

Courtesy of Tony Bates

    Fig. 12-13

Other Titles by the same Author

Children's Short Stories - Fiction

Jamie meets the Romans

Jamie meets Owain Glyndwr

Jamie meets the Vikings

Jamie meets Robin Hood

Jamie meets Blackbeard

Jamie meets William the Conquerer

Jamie meets William Shakespeare

Jamie meets Florence Nightingale

Jamie meets Robert the Bruce

Jamie meets Boudicca

Adult Fiction

Caradoc's Last Stand

Historical Reference - Non-Fiction

Little Book of Iron Age Skills

Little Book of Iron Age Warfare

Little Book of Iron Age Living